World Languages

Colours in German

Daniel Nunn

www.raintreepublishers.co.uk
Visit our website to find out more information about Raintree books.

To order:
☎ Phone 0845 6044371
🖷 Fax +44 (0) 1865 312263
🖳 Email myorders@raintreepublishers.co.uk

Customers from outside the UK please telephone +44 1865 312262

Raintree is an imprint of Capstone Global Library Limited, a company incorporated in England and Wales having its registered office at 7 Pilgrim Street, London, EC4V 6LB – Registered company number: 6695582

Text © Capstone Global Library Limited 2013
First published in hardback in 2013
The moral rights of the proprietor have been asserted.

Edited by Daniel Nunn, Rebecca Rissman, and Sian Smith
Designed by Joanna Hinton-Malivoire
Picture research by Elizabeth Alexander
Production by Alison Parsons
Originated by Capstone Global Library Ltd
Printed and bound in China by South China Printing Company Ltd

ISBN 978 1 406 23920 1
16 15 14 13 12
10 9 8 7 6 5 4 3 2 1

British Library Cataloguing in Publication Data
Nunn, Daniel.
 Colours in German. -- (World languages. Colours)
 1. German language--Vocabulary--Juvenile literature.
 2. Colors--Juvenile literature. 3. German language--
 Textbooks for foreign speakers--English.
 I. Title II. Series
 438.2'421-dc23

Acknowledgements
We would like to thank Shutterstock for permission to reproduce photographs: pp.4 (© Phiseksit), 5 (© Stephen Aaron Rees), 6 (© Tischenko Irina), 7 (© Tony Magdaraog), 8 (© szefei), 9 (© Picsfive), 10 (© Eric Isselée), 11 (© Yasonya), 12 (© Nadezhda Bolotina), 13 (© Maryna Gviazdovska), 14 (© Erik Lam), 15 (© Eric Isselée), 16 (© Ruth Black), 17 (© blueskies9), 18 (© Alexander Dashewsky), 19 (© Michele Perbellini), 20 (© Eric Isselée), 21 (© Roman Rvachov).

Cover photographs reproduced with permission of Shutterstock: dog (© Erik Lam), strawberry (© Stephen Aaron Rees), fish (© Tischenko Irina). Back cover photograph of a banana reproduced with permission of Shutterstock (© Picsfive).

We would like to thank Regina Irwin and Robert Irwin for their invaluable assistance in the preparation of this book.

Every effort has been made to contact copyright holders of material reproduced in this book. Any omissions will be rectified in subsequent printings if notice is given to the publisher.

Contents

Rot

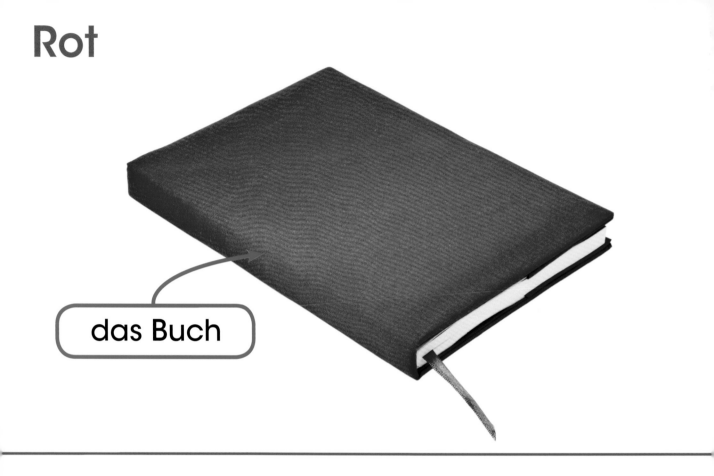

das Buch

Das Buch ist rot.

The book is red.

die Erdbeere

Die Erdbeere ist rot.

The strawberry is red.

Orange

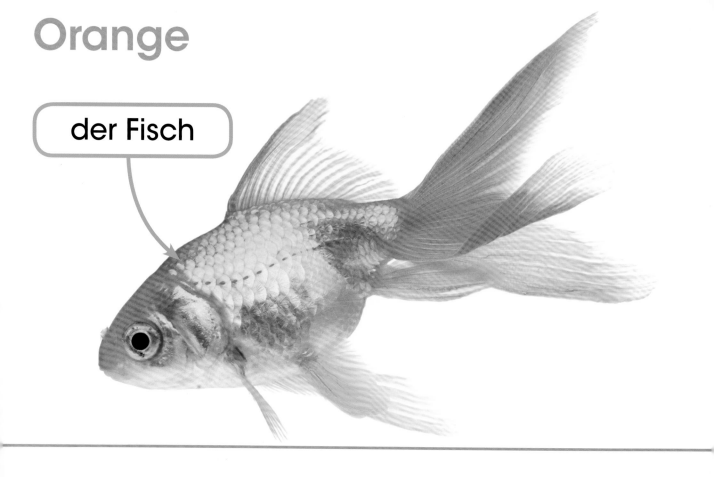

der Fisch

Der Fisch ist orange.

The fish is orange.

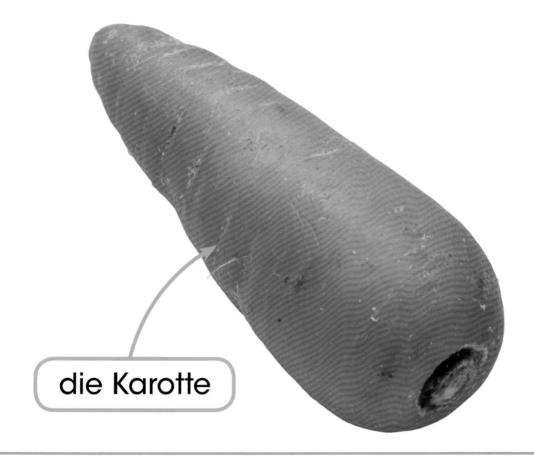

die Karotte

Die Karotte ist orange.

The carrot is orange.

Gelb

die Blume

Die Blume ist gelb.

The flower is yellow.

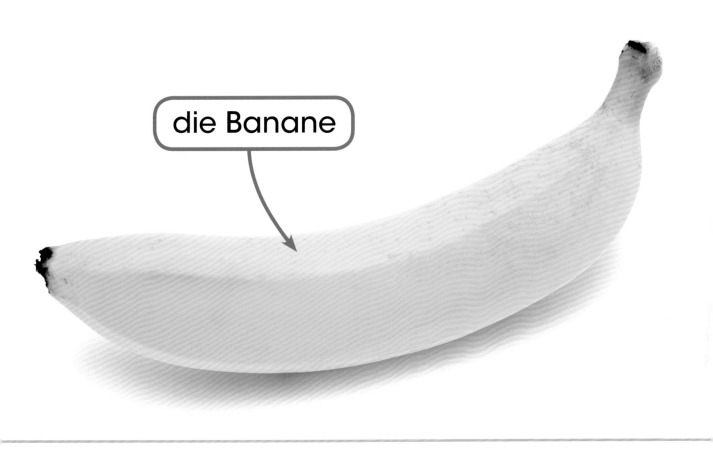

die Banane

Die Banane ist gelb.

The banana is yellow.

Grün

der Vogel

Der Vogel ist grün.

The bird is green.

der Apfel

Der Apfel ist grün.

The apple is green.

Blau

das T-shirt

Das T-shirt ist blau.

The T-shirt is blue.

die Tasse

Die Tasse ist blau.

The cup is blue.

Braun

der Hund

Der Hund ist braun.

The dog is brown.

die Kuh

Die Kuh ist braun.

The cow is brown.

Rosa

der Kuchen

Der Kuchen ist rosa.

The cake is pink.

der Hut

Der Hut ist rosa.

The hat is pink.

Weiß

die Milch

Die Milch ist weiß.

The milk is white.

der Schnee

Der Schnee ist weiß.

The snow is white.

Schwarz

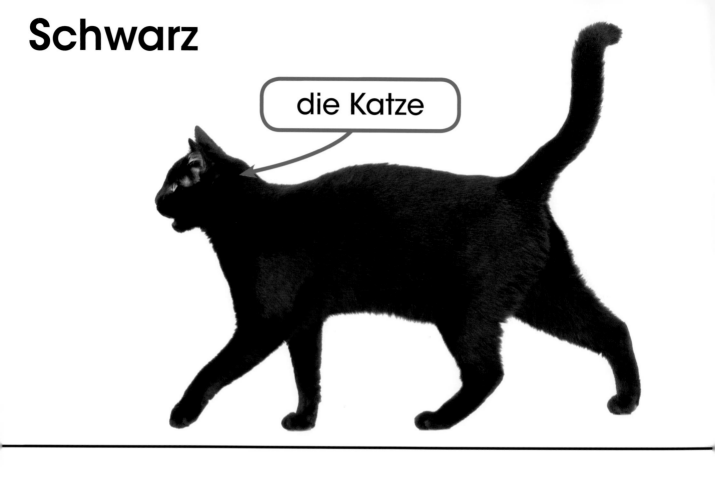

Die Katze ist **schwarz**.

The cat is **black**.

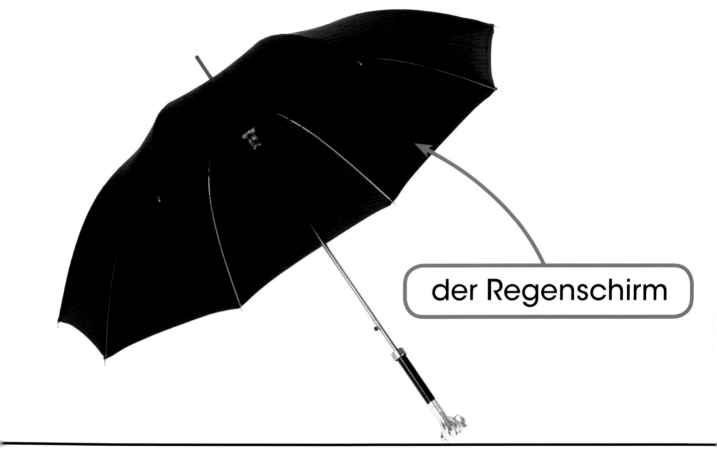

der Regenschirm

Der Regenschirm ist **schwarz**.

The umbrella is **black**.

Dictionary

German word	How to say it	English word
Apfel	ap-foll	apple
Banane	ba-na-nah	banana
blau	blou	blue
Blume	bloo-mah	flower
braun	brown	brown
Buch	boo-ch*	book
das	duss	the (neuter)
der	der	the (masculine)
die	dee	the (feminine)
Erdbeere	ert-bear-ah	strawberry
Fisch	fish	fish
gelb	gelp	yellow
grün	groon	green
Hund	hoont	dog
Hut	hoot	hat
ist	i-sst	is

German word	How to say it	English word
Karotte	ca-rot-tah	carrot
Katze	cat-zah	cat
Kuchen	koo-chen*	cake
Kuh	koo	cow
Milch	meelch*	milk
orange	o-rangah	orange
Regenschirm	reagan-sheerm	umbrella
rosa	row-sa	pink
rot	roat	red
Schnee	sh-neah	snow
schwarz	sh-wartz	black
T-shirt	t-shirt	T-shirt
Tasse	tass-ah	cup
Vogel	fo-guel	bird
weiß	wheye-ss	white

See words in the "How to say it" columns for a rough guide to pronunciations.

* Note: "ch" in German sounds like the "ch" in the Scottish word "loch".

Index

Notes for parents and teachers

In German, nouns always begin with a capital letter. Nouns are also either masculine, feminine, or neuter. The word for "the" changes accordingly – so either der (masculine), die (feminine), or das (neuter).